The Cottagecore Cookbook

AutumnRosewoodBooks@gmail.com
www.autumnrosewood.com

ISBN: 9798874037055

Cover Design by Autumn Rosewood
Printed in USA
First Printing, 2024

Welcome to The Cottagecore Cookbook, a culinary journey that beckons you into the heart of rustic charm and the simplicity of homestead living. In these pages, we invite you to explore a world where time slows down, and the kitchen becomes a haven for creating wholesome meals inspired by the beauty of nature. As the sun rises on each enchanting morning, we embrace the day with recipes that speak to the soul—Lemon Blueberry Scones that crumble with a touch, and Herbal Infusions that gently awaken the senses. Join us in cultivating a morning bliss that sets the tone for a day filled with harmony.

The Little Cottagecore Cookbook is more than a collection of recipes; it's an invitation to slow down, savor the simple moments, and infuse your kitchen with the timeless charm of cottagecore living. Join us in crafting a culinary journey that mirrors the beauty found in the heart of home.

CREATING A WHOLESOME HOMESTEAD PANTRY

Establishing a well-stocked homestead pantry is an art that harmonizes the elements of self-sufficiency, seasonality, and the pleasure of nourishing oneself with homegrown provisions. Let's delve into the specifics of each category to curate a pantry that embodies the essence of a simple and fulfilling homestead life.

1. Staple Grains and Flours:
1. Whole wheat flour for hearty baked goods
2. Cornmeal for a touch of rustic flavor
3. Rolled oats for breakfast porridge and baking
4. Quinoa for protein-rich meals
5. A variety of rice, including brown, wild, or jasmine

2. Preserved Goods:
1. Mason jars filled with homemade jams and jellies from fruits harvested on the homestead
2. Pickles and fermented vegetables for added probiotic richness
3. Canned fruits and sauces, capturing the essence of peak harvest flavors
4. Locally sourced honey and maple syrup for natural sweetness
5. Dried fruits, such as raisins, apricots, and dates, for versatile snacking and baking

3. Legumes and Pulses:
1. Dried beans like black beans, chickpeas, and lentils for protein-packed meals
2. Split peas for soups and stews
3. Homestead-grown dried peas, if cultivated

4. Baking Essentials:
1. Baking powder and baking soda for leavening
2. Yeast for homemade bread
3. A variety of sugars, including granulated, brown, and honey
4. Vanilla extract for a delightful touch of sweetness
5. Cocoa powder for chocolatey creations

5. Spices and Herbs:

- Dried herbs such as thyme, rosemary, and oregano for seasoning
- Ground spices like cinnamon, nutmeg, and cloves for aromatic warmth
- Bay leaves for savory dishes
- Salt and pepper for fundamental seasoning

6. Cooking Oils and Fats:

- Olive oil for cooking and salads
- Coconut oil for baking and high-heat cooking
- Butter, either store-bought or homemade
- Lard if raising pigs on the homestead

7. Canned Goods:

- Tomatoes in various forms (whole, crushed, diced)
- Tomato paste for concentrated flavor
- Broths, whether vegetable, chicken, or beef
- Homestead-canned soups and stews for quick and nourishing meals

8. Homestead Dairy and Eggs:

- Fresh eggs from homestead-raised chickens
- Homemade butter, churned with care
- Hard cheeses for extended storage
- Milk or milk alternatives for cooking and baking

9. Nuts and Seeds:

- Walnuts, almonds, or other homestead-grown nuts for added crunch and nutrition
- Sunflower seeds for snacking and salads
- Chia seeds and flaxseeds for added nutritional value

10. Homestead-made Preserves: - Herbal teas crafted from garden-grown herbs - Herbal tinctures and infusions for health and culinary creativity - Dried culinary herbs for a burst of flavor in dishes

11. Sweeteners: - Honey harvested from homestead beehives - Maple syrup tapped from homestead maple trees - Molasses for rich, robust sweetness

12. Homestead Harvests: - Fresh seasonal fruits and vegetables from the homestead garden - Root vegetables stored for winter use - Homestead-grown herbs, both dried and fresh

Tips for a Well-Stocked Pantry:
- **Rotation:** Regularly rotate stock to ensure freshness and prevent waste.
- **Labeling:** Clearly label and date homemade preserves for easy identification.
- **Storage:** Store grains, legumes, and flours in airtight containers to maintain quality.
- **Inventory:** Keep a record of pantry inventory for efficient meal planning and grocery shopping.

As you embark on this journey of stocking your homestead pantry, relish the connection to the land, the rhythmic dance of seasons, and the flavors that tell the story of a lifestyle rooted in simplicity and abundance. Let your pantry not only sustain you but also serve as a testament to the enduring bond between homestead and hearth.

IN THE HEART OF EVERY COUNTRY KITCHEN LIES A COLLECTION OF TIME-HONORED TOOLS, EACH WITH A PURPOSE AND HISTORY AS RICH AS THE TRADITIONS THEY SUPPORT

- **Cookware:**
  - Cast iron skillet
  - Dutch oven
  - Enamel-coated pots and pans
  - Roasting pan
- **Cutting and Chopping:**
  - High-quality chef's knife
  - Bread knife
  - Cutting board (preferably wooden)
- **Preparation:**
  - Mixing bowls (durable and varied sizes)
  - Wooden spoons and spatulas
  - Stainless steel or wooden ladle
  - Potato masher
  - Rolling pin
- **Baking:**
  - Pie plates
  - Casserole dishes
  - Baking sheets
  - Bread pans
- **Blending and Processing:**
  - Food processor
  - Hand-cranked egg beater
  - Mortar and pestle
- **Utensils:**
  - Tongs
  - Wooden-handled ladle
  - Stainless steel or wooden slotted spoon
- **Measuring:**
  - Measuring cups and spoons
  - Kitchen scale
- **Food Storage:**
  - Glass or ceramic airtight containers
  - Mason jars for preserving
  - Beeswax wraps
- **Appliances:**
  - Wood-burning stove or traditional oven
  - Hand-cranked egg beater
  - Manual coffee grinder
  - Manual can opener
- **Miscellaneous:**
  - Butter churn
  - Canning supplies (jars, lids, water bath canner)
  - Fermentation crock
  - Herb drying rack
- **Outdoor Cooking:**
  - Campfire cooking tools (grill grate, tripod)
  - Outdoor Dutch oven for open-flame cooking
- **Textiles:**
  - Vintage-style apron
  - Dish towels and cloths
  - Oven mitts

A CULINARY MEADOW

MORNING BLISS

Awaken your senses with enchanting recipes like
Lemon Blueberry Scones and soothing Herbal
Infusions that set the tone for a delightful day.

GARDEN FRESH START

Dive into vibrant flavors with recipes such as Caprese
Avocado Toast, Sunrise Smoothie Bowls, all inspired by
the goodness of garden-fresh ingredients.

PICNIC DELIGHTS

Pack a perfect picnic basket with recipes like Herb and
Cream Cheese Cucumber Sandwiches, Mason Jar Pasta
Salad, and refreshing Homemade Lemonade, creating a
picnic experience that captures the essence of outdoor bliss.

SIP OF NATURE

Explore refreshing beverage recipes like Honey
Lavender Lemonade, Fruit-Infused Iced Tea, and
Homemade Herbal Soda, inviting you to savor the
simplicity of nature's flavors.

HARVEST FEAST

Delight in heartwarming dishes such as Honey
Lavender Roasted Chicken, Maple Balsamic Glazed
Brussels Sprouts, and a comforting Hearty Lentil
Soup that embodies the spirit of a bountiful harvest.

BREADS AND SPREADS

Master the art of creating rustic bread with the
Sourdough Starter Guide, complemented by recipes
like Honey Oat Bread and Homemade Butter for a
perfect bread-and-spread experience.

SWEET MOMENTS

Indulge your sweet tooth with treats like Rose Petal
and Raspberry Jam Thumbprint Cookies, Rustic
Berry Galette, and wholesome Maple Walnut Oat
Bars, inviting you to savor every delightful moment.

COZY CONFECTIONS

Bake with love using recipes like Vanilla Lavender Cake,
Chocolate-Dipped Almond Biscotti, and Rosemary
Lemon Olive Oil Cake, creating confections that radiate
comfort and charm.

PRESERVES AND SWEETS

Learn the art of preserving with recipes for Homestead
Apple Butter, Homemade Strawberry Jam, and Orange
Cardamom Marmalade, ensuring a taste of sweetness all year
round.

SAVOR THE SEASONS

Celebrate the changing seasons with Peach and Berry
Cobbler, Harvest Pumpkin Muffins, and Spiced Apple
Cider Donuts, embracing the cyclical beauty of nature.

MORNING BLISS

L E M O N B L U E B E R R Y S C O N E S

- Ingredients:
  - 2 cups all-purpose flour
  - 1/2 cup granulated sugar
  - 1 tablespoon baking powder
  - 1/2 teaspoon salt
  - 1/2 cup unsalted butter, cold and cubed
  - 1 cup fresh blueberries
  - 1/2 cup milk
  - 1 teaspoon vanilla extract
  - Zest of 1 lemon
  - Optional: Powdered sugar for dusting

- Instructions:
  - Preheat the oven to 400°F (200°C). Line a baking sheet with parchment paper.
  - In a large bowl, whisk together flour, sugar, baking powder, and salt.
  - Add the cold, cubed butter and use a pastry cutter to cut it into the flour until the mixture resembles coarse crumbs.
  - Gently fold in the blueberries.
  - In a separate bowl, whisk together milk, vanilla extract, and lemon zest. Add the wet ingredients to the dry ingredients and stir until just combined.
  - Turn the dough out onto a floured surface and shape it into a circle. Cut into wedges and place them on the prepared baking sheet.
  - Bake for 15-18 minutes or until the scones are golden brown. Optional: Dust with powdered sugar before serving.

VANILLA CINNAMON WAFFLES

Ingredients:
- 2 cups all-purpose flour
- 2 tablespoons sugar
- 1 tablespoon baking powder
- 1/2 teaspoon salt
- 1 3/4 cups milk
- 1/3 cup vegetable oil
- 2 large eggs
- 1 teaspoon vanilla extract
- 1/2 teaspoon ground cinnamon
- Butter and maple syrup for serving

Instructions:
1. **Preheat Waffle Iron:**
   - Preheat your waffle iron according to the manufacturer's instructions.
2. **Prepare Dry Ingredients:**
   - In a large mixing bowl, whisk together the flour, sugar, baking powder, and salt.
3. **Combine Wet Ingredients:**
   - In a separate bowl, whisk together the milk, vegetable oil, eggs, vanilla extract, and ground cinnamon.
4. **Mix Batter:**
   - Pour the wet ingredients into the dry ingredients and gently stir until just combined. Be careful not to overmix; it's okay if there are a few lumps.
5. **Cook Waffles:**
   - Lightly grease the waffle iron with non-stick cooking spray or a small amount of melted butter. Pour enough batter to cover the waffle grid and close the lid. Cook according to the manufacturer's instructions until the waffles are golden brown.
6. **Serve Warm:**
   - Carefully remove the waffles from the iron and serve them warm. Top with a pat of butter and drizzle with maple syrup.
7. **Optional Garnish:**
   - For an extra touch of cottagecore charm, you can garnish the waffles with fresh berries, a sprinkle of powdered sugar, or a dollop of whipped cream.

HERBAL INFUSIONS FOR BREAKFAST

- Lavender Chamomile Tea:
  - Ingredients:
    - 1 tablespoon dried lavender buds
    - 1 tablespoon dried chamomile flowers
    - 2 cups hot water
  - Instructions:
    - Combine dried lavender buds and chamomile flowers in a teapot or infuser.
    - Pour hot water over the herbs and let steep for 5-7 minutes.
    - Strain and serve.
- Rosemary Mint Infusion:
  - Ingredients:
    - 1 tablespoon fresh rosemary leaves
    - 1 tablespoon fresh mint leaves
    - 2 cups hot water
  - Instructions:
    - Bruise the rosemary and mint leaves to release their flavors.
    - Place the leaves in a teapot or infuser.
    - Pour hot water over the leaves and let steep for 5-7 minutes.
    - Strain and enjoy.

COTTAGECORE FRITTATA WITH HERBS

- Ingredients:
    - 6 large eggs
    - 1/4 cup milk
    - Salt and pepper to taste
    - 1 tablespoon butter
    - 1 cup cherry tomatoes, halved
    - 1/2 cup feta cheese, crumbled
    - 2 tablespoons fresh basil, chopped
    - 1 tablespoon fresh chives, chopped
    -
- Instructions:
    - Preheat the oven to 375°F (190°C).
    - In a bowl, whisk together eggs, milk, salt, and pepper.
    - In an oven-safe skillet, melt butter over medium heat.
    - Pour the egg mixture into the skillet.
    - Scatter cherry tomatoes, feta cheese, basil, and chives evenly over the eggs.
    - Cook on the stovetop for 2-3 minutes until the edges start to set.
    - Transfer the skillet to the preheated oven and bake for 12-15 minutes or until the frittata is set in the middle.
    - Slice into wedges and serve warm for a hearty morning delight.

FLUFFY LEMON RICOTTA PANCAKES

- Ingredients:
  - 1 cup all-purpose flour
  - 1 tablespoon sugar
  - 1 teaspoon baking powder
  - 1/2 teaspoon baking soda
  - 1/4 teaspoon salt
  - 1 cup ricotta cheese
  - 2/3 cup milk
  - 2 large eggs
  - Zest of 1 lemon
  - Butter for cooking
  - Maple syrup for serving
  -
- Instructions:
  - In a large bowl, whisk together flour, sugar, baking powder, baking soda, and salt.
  - In a separate bowl, combine ricotta cheese, milk, eggs, and lemon zest. Mix until smooth.
  - Add the wet ingredients to the dry ingredients and stir until just combined.
  - Heat a griddle or non-stick skillet over medium heat and lightly grease with butter.
  - Pour 1/4 cup portions of batter onto the griddle and cook until bubbles form on the surface. Flip and cook until golden brown.
  - Serve with a drizzle of maple syrup.

ORANGE BLOSSOM FRENCH TOAST

- Ingredients:
    - 4 slices thick-cut bread
    - 2 large eggs
    - 1/2 cup milk
    - Zest of 1 orange
    - 1 tablespoon orange blossom water
    - 1/2 teaspoon vanilla extract
    - Butter for cooking
    - Maple syrup and powdered sugar for serving

- Instructions:
    - In a shallow bowl, whisk together eggs, milk, orange zest, orange blossom water, and vanilla extract.
    - Dip each slice of bread into the egg mixture, ensuring both sides are well-coated.
    - Heat butter in a skillet over medium heat and cook the bread slices until golden brown on both sides.
    - Serve with a drizzle of maple syrup and a sprinkle of powdered sugar.

APPLE CINNAMON OVERNIGHT OATS

- Ingredients:
  - 1/2 cup rolled oats
  - 1/2 cup milk (dairy or plant-based)
  - 1/2 cup unsweetened applesauce
  - 1 tablespoon maple syrup
  - 1/2 teaspoon ground cinnamon
  - 1/2 apple, diced
  - Chopped nuts for topping

- Instructions:
  - In a jar or container, combine rolled oats, milk, applesauce, maple syrup, and ground cinnamon.
  - Stir well, add diced apples, and refrigerate overnight.
  - In the morning, give the oats a good stir and top with chopped nuts before serving.

BUCKWHEAT PORRIDGE WITH APPLES AND CINNAMON

Ingredients:

- 1/2 cup buckwheat groats
- 1 cup milk (dairy or plant-based)
- 1 cup water
- 1 apple, peeled and diced
- 1 tablespoon honey or maple syrup
- 1/2 teaspoon ground cinnamon

Instructions:

1. In a saucepan, combine buckwheat groats, milk, water, diced apple, honey or maple syrup, and ground cinnamon.
2. Bring to a boil, then reduce the heat to low, cover, and simmer for 15-20 minutes or until the buckwheat is tender and the porridge thickens.
3. Stir occasionally, and add more liquid if needed.
4. Serve warm with additional diced apples and a sprinkle of cinnamon.

Feel free to get creative with your porridge recipes by adding your favorite fruits, nuts, seeds, or spices. Porridge is a canvas for delicious and nutritious breakfast creations!

HOMESTEAD HASH BROWNS WITH HERBS

- Ingredients:
  - 4 large potatoes, peeled and grated
  - 1 onion, finely chopped
  - 2 tablespoons olive oil
  - 1 teaspoon dried thyme
  - Salt and pepper to taste
  - Fresh parsley, chopped, for garnish

- Instructions:
  - Place grated potatoes in a clean kitchen towel and squeeze out excess moisture.
  - In a large skillet, heat olive oil over medium heat. Add chopped onion and cook until translucent.
  - Add grated potatoes to the skillet, spreading them out evenly.
  - Sprinkle dried thyme, salt, and pepper over the potatoes. Allow them to cook without stirring until the bottom is golden brown.
  - Flip the potatoes and continue cooking until the other side is golden brown and crispy.
  - Garnish with fresh parsley and serve hot.

GARDEN FRESH START

HOMEMADE HERB BAGELS WITH CREAMY HERB SPREAD

- **Ingredients (Bagels):**
  - 3 1/2 cups all-purpose flour
  - 1 tablespoon sugar
  - 1 teaspoon salt
  - 1 tablespoon fresh herbs (rosemary, thyme, chives), chopped
  - 1 packet (2 1/4 teaspoons) active dry yeast
  - 1 1/4 cups warm water
- **Ingredients (Creamy Herb Spread):**
  - Cream cheese
  - Fresh herbs (dill, chives, parsley), chopped
  - Salt and pepper to taste
- **Instructions:**
  - In a bowl, combine flour, sugar, salt, and chopped herbs.
  - Dissolve yeast in warm water and let it sit for 5 minutes until frothy.
  - Mix the yeast mixture into the dry ingredients and knead until a smooth dough forms.
  - Divide the dough into equal portions and shape into bagels. Let them rise for 1 hour.
  - Preheat the oven to 425°F (220°C). Boil the bagels briefly in water, then bake until golden brown.
  - Mix cream cheese with fresh herbs, salt, and pepper for the spread.
  - Spread the herby cream cheese on the freshly baked bagels.

HOMEMADE GRANOLA

- **Ingredients:**
  - 3 cups old-fashioned oats
  - 1 cup nuts (almonds, walnuts), chopped
  - 1/2 cup seeds (sunflower, pumpkin)
  - 1/2 cup dried fruit (raisins, cranberries)
  - 1/4 cup coconut oil, melted
  - 1/4 cup honey or maple syrup
  - 1 teaspoon vanilla extract
  - 1/2 teaspoon cinnamon
  - Pinch of salt

- **Instructions:**
  - Preheat the oven to 325°F (163°C). Line a baking sheet with parchment paper.
  - In a large bowl, combine oats, chopped nuts, seeds, and dried fruit.
  - In a separate bowl, whisk together melted coconut oil, honey or maple syrup, vanilla extract, cinnamon, and a pinch of salt.
  - Pour the wet ingredients over the dry ingredients and toss until well coated.
  - Spread the mixture evenly on the prepared baking sheet.
  - Bake for 20-25 minutes, stirring halfway through, until golden brown.

Allow to cool completely before storing in an airtight container.

CAPRESE AVOCADO TOAST

Ingredients:
- 2 slices whole-grain bread, toasted
- 1 ripe avocado, mashed
- 1 large tomato, sliced
- Fresh mozzarella, sliced
- Fresh basil leaves
- Balsamic glaze
- Salt and pepper

Instructions:
1. **Toast Bread:**
   - Toast whole-grain bread slices until golden brown.
2. **Assemble:**
   - Spread mashed avocado on each slice.
3. **Layer:**
   - Add tomato slices, fresh mozzarella, and basil leaves.
4. **Season:**
   - Sprinkle with salt and pepper.
5. **Drizzle:**
   - Finish with a drizzle of balsamic glaze.
6. **Serve:**
   - Serve immediately for a delightful Caprese Avocado Toast.

SUNRISE SMOOTHIE BOWL

Ingredients:
- 2 frozen bananas
- 1 cup frozen mixed berries (strawberries, blueberries, raspberries)
- 1/2 cup Greek yogurt
- 1/4 cup almond milk
- Toppings: Granola, sliced bananas, chia seeds, edible flowers

Instructions:
1. **Gather Ingredients:**
   - Ensure bananas are frozen. Have frozen mixed berries, Greek yogurt, almond milk, and toppings ready.
2. **Blend the Smoothie Base:**
   - In a blender, combine frozen bananas, frozen mixed berries, Greek yogurt, and almond milk.
3. **Blend Until Smooth:**
   - Blend the ingredients until you achieve a smooth and creamy consistency. Add more almond milk if needed.
4. **Prepare Toppings:**
   - Gather granola, sliced bananas, chia seeds, and edible flowers for toppings.
5. **Pour into Bowl:**
   - Pour the smoothie into a bowl, spreading it evenly.
6. **Add Toppings:**
   - Arrange granola, sliced bananas, and chia seeds on top of the smoothie base.
7. **Decorate with Edible Flowers:**
   - For a visually appealing touch, delicately place edible flowers on the smoothie bowl.
8. **Serve Immediately:**
   - Enjoy the Sunrise Smoothie Bowl immediately for a refreshing and nutritious start to your day.

SUNDRIED TOMATO AND BASIL QUICHE

- **Ingredients (Quiche Filling):**
  - 1 pie crust (store-bought or homemade)
  - 4 large eggs
  - 1 cup milk
  - 1 cup cherry tomatoes, halved
  - 1/2 cup sundried tomatoes, chopped
  - 1/4 cup fresh basil, chopped
  - 1 cup shredded mozzarella cheese
  - Salt and pepper to taste

- **Instructions:**
  - Preheat the oven to 375°F (190°C).
  - In a bowl, whisk together eggs, milk, salt, and pepper.
  - Roll out the pie crust and place it in a pie dish.
  - Layer cherry tomatoes, sundried tomatoes, and fresh basil in the crust.
  - Pour the egg mixture over the tomatoes and basil.
  - Sprinkle shredded mozzarella on top.
  - Bake for 35-40 minutes or until the quiche is set and golden brown.

COTTAGE GARDEN FRUIT SALAD

Ingredients:
- 1 cup watermelon, cubed
- 1 cup cantaloupe, cubed
- 1 cup strawberries, halved
- 1 cup blueberries
- 2 kiwis, sliced
- Fresh mint and basil, chopped
- Honey for drizzling

Instructions:
1. **Prepare Fruits:**
   - Cube watermelon and cantaloupe.
   - Halve strawberries.
   - Slice kiwis.
2. **Combine Fruits:**
   - In a bowl, mix watermelon, cantaloupe, strawberries, blueberries, and kiwis.
3. **Add Fresh Herbs:**
   - Sprinkle chopped mint and basil over fruits.
4. **Gently Toss:**
   - Toss gently to combine, avoiding crushing delicate fruits.
5. **Drizzle with Honey:**
   - Drizzle honey over the fruit mixture.
6. **Serve:**
   - Spoon into bowls or onto a platter.
7. **Optional Chill:**
   - Refrigerate for 30 minutes for a chilled option.
8. **Garnish (Optional):**
   - Garnish with additional mint and basil leaves.
9. **Enjoy:**
   - Serve as a refreshing breakfast or snack.

AUTUMN ORCHARD SALAD WITH MAPLE PECAN VINAIGRETTE

Ingredients:

For the Salad:
- 6 cups mixed salad greens (baby spinach, romaine, and red leaf lettuce)
- 1 medium apple, thinly sliced
- 1/2 cup dried cranberries
- 1/2 cup crumbled blue cheese or goat cheese
- 1/2 cup candied pecans, roughly chopped
- 1/4 cup red onion, thinly sliced
- Sliced pear for garnish (optional)

For the Maple Pecan Vinaigrette:
- 3 tablespoons extra-virgin olive oil
- 2 tablespoons apple cider vinegar
- 1 tablespoon pure maple syrup
- 1 teaspoon Dijon mustard
- 1/4 cup chopped candied pecans
- Salt and pepper to taste
-

Instructions:

- **Prepare the Autumn Orchard Salad:**
  - In a large salad bowl, combine the mixed greens, thinly sliced apple, dried cranberries, crumbled blue cheese, candied pecans, and red onion.

- **Make the Maple Pecan Vinaigrette:**
  - In a small blender or food processor, blend together the olive oil, apple cider vinegar, maple syrup, Dijon mustard, chopped candied pecans, salt, and pepper until smooth.

- **Dress the Salad:**
  - Drizzle the maple pecan vinaigrette over the salad and toss gently to ensure each bite is coated in the delightful flavors.

- **Garnish with Sliced Pear (Optional):**
  - For an extra touch of sweetness and texture, garnish the salad with thinly sliced pear.

- **Serve and Enjoy the Orchard Bliss:**
  - Divide the salad into individual plates, appreciating the vibrant colors and rich textures that evoke the essence of an autumn orchard. Revel in the delightful combination of crisp apples, tart cranberries, creamy cheese, and the crunch of candied pecans.

PICNIC
DELIGHTS

SAVORY HERB AND CREAM CHEESE CUCUMBER SANDWICHES

Ingredients:

- 8 slices of your favorite bread (white, whole wheat, or a rustic country loaf)
- 1 large cucumber, thinly sliced
- 1/2 cup cream cheese, softened
- 2 tablespoons fresh dill, finely chopped
- 1 tablespoon fresh chives, minced
- 1 teaspoon lemon zest
- Salt and black pepper to taste
- Butter, softened (for spreading on bread)

Instructions:

1. **Prepare the Cream Cheese Spread:**
   - In a mixing bowl, combine the softened cream cheese, fresh dill, minced chives, and lemon zest.
   - Season with salt and black pepper to taste.
   - Mix well until the herbs are evenly distributed.
2. **Slice the Cucumber:**
   - Thinly slice the cucumber into rounds. You can use a mandoline for precision.
3. **Assemble the Sandwiches:**
   - Spread a generous layer of the herb-infused cream cheese on one side of each bread slice.
   - Arrange a layer of thinly sliced cucumbers over the cream cheese on half of the bread slices.
   - Place the remaining slices of bread, cream cheese side down, on top of the cucumbers to create sandwiches.
4. **Trim and Cut:**
   - Trim the crusts off the sandwiches for a neater look, if desired.
   - Cut the sandwiches into halves or quarters, creating finger-sized or bite-sized portions perfect for picnics.
5. **Serve and Enjoy:**
   - Arrange the sandwiches on a serving platter or pack them in your picnic basket.

MASON JAR PASTA SALAD

- Ingredients:

    - 2 cups cooked pasta (rotini or fusilli work well)
    - 1 cup cherry tomatoes, halved
    - 1/2 cup cucumber, diced
    - 1/4 cup red onion, finely chopped
    - 1/4 cup black olives, sliced
    - 1/4 cup feta cheese, crumbled
    - 2 tablespoons fresh basil, chopped
    - 3 tablespoons olive oil
    - 2 tablespoons balsamic vinegar
    - Salt and pepper to taste

- Instructions:

    - In a mason jar, layer cooked pasta, cherry tomatoes, cucumber, red onion, black olives, feta cheese, and fresh basil.
    - In a small bowl, whisk together olive oil, balsamic vinegar, salt, and pepper.
    - Pour the dressing over the salad in the mason jar.
    - Seal the jar and refrigerate until ready to serve.
    - Shake well before serving.

SAVORY HERB BISCUITS WITH COUNTRY HAM

Ingredients:
- 2 cups all-purpose flour
- 1 tablespoon baking powder
- 1/2 teaspoon baking soda
- 1 teaspoon salt
- 1/2 cup unsalted butter, cold and cubed
- 1 cup buttermilk
- 2 tablespoons fresh herbs (such as chives, thyme, or rosemary), chopped
- Thin slices of country ham

Instructions:

1. Preheat and Prepare:
   - Preheat the oven to 425°F (220°C). Line a baking sheet with parchment paper.
2. Mix Dry Ingredients:
   - In a large bowl, whisk together flour, baking powder, baking soda, and salt.
3. Cut in Butter:
   - Add cold, cubed butter to the flour mixture. Use your fingers to rub the butter into the flour until it resembles coarse crumbs.
4. Add Buttermilk and Herbs:
   - Pour in the buttermilk and add the chopped herbs. Mix until just combined.
5. Shape and Cut:
   - Turn the dough onto a floured surface and pat into a rectangle.
   - Cut out biscuits using a round cutter.
6. Bake:
   - Place the biscuits on the prepared baking sheet and bake for 12-15 minutes or until golden.
7. Serve:
   - Let the biscuits cool slightly before slicing and filling with thin slices of country ham.

HERBED CHICKEN SANDWICHES

- Ingredients:

  - Cooked and shredded chicken (rotisserie chicken works well)
  - Mayonnaise
  - Dijon mustard
  - Fresh herbs (parsley, dill, chives), chopped
  - Salt and pepper to taste
  - Bread or rolls for sandwiches
  - Lettuce leaves and tomato slices for assembling

- Instructions:

  - In a bowl, mix shredded chicken with mayonnaise, Dijon mustard, chopped herbs, salt, and pepper.
  - Spread the chicken mixture on slices of bread or rolls.
  - Top with lettuce leaves and tomato slices.
  - Assemble the sandwiches and cut into halves for easy serving.

WILDFLOWER CHICKPEA SALAD

Ingredients:
- 2 cans (15 oz each) chickpeas, drained and rinsed
- 1 cup cherry tomatoes, halved
- 1 cup cucumber, diced
- 1/2 cup red onion, finely chopped
- 1/4 cup crumbled feta cheese
- 1/4 cup Kalamata olives, sliced
- 1/4 cup fresh dill, chopped
- 1/4 cup fresh basil leaves, torn
- 2 tablespoons extra-virgin olive oil
- Juice of 1 lemon
- Salt and black pepper to taste

Instructions:
1. **Prepare Chickpeas:**
   - Rinse and drain the chickpeas, then pat them dry with a paper towel.
2. **Combine Ingredients:**
   - In a large bowl, combine chickpeas, cherry tomatoes, cucumber, red onion, feta cheese, Kalamata olives, fresh dill, and torn basil leaves.
3. **Make Lemon Herb Dressing:**
   - In a small bowl, whisk together extra-virgin olive oil, lemon juice, salt, and black pepper.
4. **Drizzle and Toss:**
   - Drizzle the lemon herb dressing over the salad and toss gently to combine.
5. **Chill:**
   - Allow the salad to chill in the refrigerator for at least 1 hour to enhance the flavors.
6. **Serve:**
   - Serve this Wildflower Chickpea Salad as a light and protein-packed option for your picnic.

CLASSIC HOMEMADE LEMONADE

Ingredients:

- 1 cup freshly squeezed lemon juice (about 4-6 lemons)
- 1 cup granulated sugar (adjust to taste)
- 5 cups cold water
- Ice cubes
- Lemon slices for garnish
- Fresh mint leaves (optional)

Instructions:

1. **Make Lemon Syrup:**
   - In a small saucepan, combine 1 cup of water and the granulated sugar. Heat over medium heat, stirring occasionally, until the sugar completely dissolves. This creates a simple syrup.
2. **Squeeze Lemons:**
   - While the syrup is cooling, squeeze enough lemons to get 1 cup of freshly squeezed lemon juice.
3. **Combine Lemon Juice and Syrup:**
   - In a pitcher, combine the freshly squeezed lemon juice and the simple syrup. Stir well to mix.
4. **Add Cold Water:**
   - Pour in the remaining 4 cups of cold water and stir until well combined.
5. **Adjust Sweetness:**
   - Taste the lemonade and adjust the sweetness by adding more sugar if needed. Stir until the sugar is fully dissolved.
6. **Chill:**
   - Place the pitcher in the refrigerator to chill the lemonade.
7. **Serve Over Ice:**
   - When ready to serve, fill glasses with ice cubes and pour the chilled lemonade over the ice.
8. **Garnish (Optional):**
   - Garnish each glass with a slice of lemon and a sprig of fresh mint for a decorative touch.
9. **Enjoy:**
   - Sip and enjoy the refreshing goodness of homemade lemonade!

SIP OF
NATURE

HOMEMADE HERBAL SODA

Ingredients:
For the Herbal Syrup:
- 1 cup water
- 1 cup granulated sugar
- 1/2 cup fresh herbs (such as mint, basil, or rosemary), loosely packed

For the Soda:
- Sparkling water
- Ice cubes
- Fresh herbs and citrus slices for garnish

Instructions:

1. Prepare the Herbal Syrup:
- In a small saucepan, combine water, sugar, and fresh herbs.
- Heat the mixture over medium heat, stirring until the sugar dissolves.
- Once the mixture comes to a gentle boil, reduce heat and simmer for about 5 minutes.
- Remove the saucepan from heat and let the herbal syrup cool completely.
- Strain the syrup to remove the herbs, leaving you with a flavorful herbal-infused syrup.

2. Assemble the Homemade Herbal Soda:
- Fill glasses with ice cubes.
- Pour 2-3 tablespoons of the herbal syrup into each glass, depending on your sweetness preference.
- Top with sparkling water to fill the glass.
- Stir gently to combine the syrup and sparkling water.
- Garnish with fresh herbs and citrus slices.

3. Enjoy:
Sip and enjoy your Homemade Herbal Soda! Experiment with different herbal combinations to find your favorite flavor. It's a delightful and natural alternative to store-bought sodas, perfect for a picnic or any outdoor gathering.

FRUIT-INFUSED ICED TEA

Ingredients:

For the Tea:
- 4 cups water
- 4-6 tea bags (black, green, or herbal tea of your choice)

For the Fruit Infusion:
- 1 cup fresh fruit slices (such as berries, citrus, peaches, or a combination)
- 1-2 tablespoons honey or agave syrup (optional, for sweetness)
- Fresh mint leaves for garnish (optional)

For Serving:
- Ice cubes

Instructions:

1. Brew the Tea:
- Bring 4 cups of water to a boil in a saucepan.
- Remove the saucepan from heat, add the tea bags, and let them steep for 5-7 minutes. Adjust the steeping time based on your tea variety and desired strength.
- Remove the tea bags and allow the brewed tea to cool to room temperature.

2. Prepare the Fruit Infusion:
- In a pitcher, combine the brewed tea with fresh fruit slices.
- Add honey or agave syrup if you prefer a sweeter taste. Adjust the sweetness to your liking.
- Stir the mixture well to combine the flavors.
- Refrigerate the pitcher for at least 2 hours to allow the fruit flavors to infuse into the tea.

3. Serve the Fruit-Infused Iced Tea:
- Fill glasses with ice cubes.
- Pour the fruit-infused tea over the ice.
- Garnish with fresh mint leaves if desired.

4. Enjoy:
Sip and savor the delightful flavors of this Fruit-Infused Iced Tea. It's a beautiful and refreshing drink that captures the essence of nature, making it a perfect addition to your Cottagecore-inspired moments.

HONEY LAVENDER LEMONADE

:

Ingredients:
- 1 cup fresh lemon juice (about 6-8 lemons)
- 1/2 cup honey (adjust to taste)
- 1 tablespoon dried culinary lavender buds
- 6 cups cold water
- Ice cubes
- Fresh lavender sprigs and lemon slices for garnish (optional)

Instructions:

1. Make Lavender Infused Honey:
- In a small saucepan, combine honey and dried lavender buds.
- Heat the mixture over low heat, stirring until the honey becomes liquid and infused with lavender. Be careful not to boil the honey.
- Remove from heat and let the lavender honey cool. Strain the lavender buds from the honey using a fine mesh strainer.

2. Prepare the Lemonade:
- In a pitcher, combine fresh lemon juice, lavender-infused honey, and cold water.
- Stir the mixture well to ensure the honey is fully dissolved.
- Taste the lemonade and adjust the sweetness by adding more honey if needed.

3. Chill and Serve:
- Refrigerate the pitcher for at least 1-2 hours to allow the flavors to meld.
- Before serving, stir the lemonade and adjust sweetness if necessary.

4. Serve with Garnishes:
- Fill glasses with ice cubes.
- Pour the chilled Honey Lavender Lemonade over the ice.
- Garnish with fresh lavender sprigs and lemon slices if desired.

5. Enjoy:
Sip and enjoy the aromatic and soothing flavors of this Honey Lavender Lemonade.

CHAI SPICED APPLE CIDER

Ingredients:

- 4 cups apple cider
- 2 chai tea bags
- 1 cinnamon stick
- 4 whole cloves
- 1 orange peel (strips)
- Honey or maple syrup to taste
- Whipped cream and ground cinnamon for garnish (optional)

Instructions:

1. In a saucepan, heat apple cider until it simmers.
2. Add chai tea bags, cinnamon stick, whole cloves, and orange peel.
3. Allow the mixture to simmer for 10-15 minutes to infuse the flavors.
4. Remove tea bags and spices. Sweeten with honey or maple syrup to taste.
5. Pour into mugs and garnish with a dollop of whipped cream and a sprinkle of ground cinnamon if desired.
6. Serve warm and enjoy the cozy blend of apple and chai spices.

MAPLE LAVENDER LATTE

Ingredients:
- 1 cup milk (dairy or plant-based)
- 1 tablespoon dried culinary lavender buds
- 1-2 shots of espresso or 1/2 cup strong brewed coffee
- 1-2 tablespoons maple syrup
- Lavender sugar for rimming (optional)
- Dried lavender buds for garnish (optional)

Instructions:

For Lavender-Infused Milk:
- In a small saucepan, heat the milk until it's warm but not boiling.
- Add dried culinary lavender buds to the warm milk and let it steep for 5-7 minutes.
- Strain the lavender buds from the milk and return the infused milk to the saucepan.

For the Latte:
- Brew espresso or strong coffee.
- Whisk the lavender-infused milk until it becomes frothy, or use a milk frother.
- Pour the brewed espresso or coffee into a mug.
- Pour the lavender-infused frothy milk over the espresso or coffee.
- Stir in maple syrup to sweeten, adjusting to taste.

Optional Garnishes:
- Rim the edge of the mug with lavender sugar for an extra touch of sweetness and aroma.
- Garnish with a sprinkle of dried lavender buds on top.

Sip and savor the delightful combination of floral lavender, sweet maple, and rich espresso in this Maple Lavender Latte. It's a warm and comforting drink perfect for quiet moments of relaxation.

CINNAMON MAPLE ALMOND MILK LATTE

Ingredients:
- 1 cup almond milk
- 1/2 teaspoon ground cinnamon
- 1-2 shots of espresso or 1/2 cup strong brewed coffee
- 1-2 tablespoons maple syrup
- Ground cinnamon for garnish

Instructions:
- In a small saucepan, heat almond milk until warm but not boiling.
- Whisk in ground cinnamon and maple syrup until well combined.
- Brew espresso or strong coffee.
- Pour the brewed espresso or coffee into a mug.
- Pour the cinnamon maple almond milk over the espresso or coffee.
- Sprinkle with ground cinnamon for garnish.
- Stir and enjoy the comforting and subtly sweet flavors.

These warm and inviting beverages provide a comforting and aromatic experience inspired by the beauty of nature. Each sip is a journey into the soothing elements of herbal, spicy, and sweet notes. Enjoy these drinks during cozy moments by the fire or when you need a bit of warmth and relaxation.

HARVEST
FEAST

BUTTERNUT SQUASH RISOTTO

Ingredients:
- 1 butternut squash, peeled, seeded, and diced
- 2 cups Arborio rice
- 1 onion, finely chopped
- 4 cups vegetable broth, heated
- 1 cup dry white wine
- 1/2 cup Parmesan cheese, grated
- 4 tablespoons butter
- 2 tablespoons olive oil
- Salt and pepper to taste
- Fresh sage leaves for garnish

Instructions:

1. **Roast Butternut Squash:**
   - Preheat the oven to 400°F (200°C). Toss the diced butternut squash with olive oil, salt, and pepper. Roast until tender and slightly caramelized.
2. **Sauté Onion:**
   - In a large skillet, sauté the finely chopped onion in olive oil until translucent.
3. **Add Rice:**
   - Stir in Arborio rice and cook for a couple of minutes until the rice is lightly toasted.
4. **Deglaze with Wine:**
   - Pour in the dry white wine, stirring constantly until the liquid is mostly absorbed.
5. **Add Broth:**
   - Begin adding the heated vegetable broth, one ladle at a time, stirring frequently. Allow the liquid to be absorbed before adding more.
6. **Continue Cooking:**
   - Repeat the process until the rice is creamy and cooked to al dente. This usually takes about 18-20 minutes.
7. **Fold in Butternut Squash:**
   - Gently fold in the roasted butternut squash, Parmesan cheese, and butter. Season with salt and pepper to taste.
8. **Serve:**
   - Garnish with fresh sage leaves and serve warm.

HEARTY LENTIL SOUP

Ingredients:

- 1 cup dried green or brown lentils, rinsed and drained
- 1 onion, finely chopped
- 2 carrots, diced
- 2 celery stalks, diced
- 3 cloves garlic, minced
- 1 can (14 oz) diced tomatoes
- 6 cups vegetable broth
- 1 cup kale or spinach, chopped
- 1 teaspoon ground cumin
- 1 teaspoon ground coriander
- 1/2 teaspoon smoked paprika
- 1 bay leaf
- Salt and pepper to taste
- 2 tablespoons olive oil
- Fresh parsley for garnish
- Lemon wedges for serving

Instructions:

- **Sauté Vegetables:**
  - In a large pot, heat olive oil over medium heat. Add chopped onions, carrots, and celery. Sauté until the vegetables are softened, about 5-7 minutes.
- **Add Garlic and Spices:**
  - Stir in minced garlic, ground cumin, ground coriander, smoked paprika, salt, and pepper. Cook for an additional 2 minutes, allowing the spices to become fragrant.

- **Add Lentils and Broth:**
  - Add rinsed lentils, diced tomatoes, vegetable broth, and the bay leaf to the pot. Bring the mixture to a boil.
- **Simmer:**
  - Reduce heat to low, cover, and let the soup simmer for 25-30 minutes or until the lentils are tender.
- **Add Greens:**
  - Stir in chopped kale or spinach during the last 5 minutes of cooking, allowing the greens to wilt.
- **Adjust Seasoning:**
  - Taste the soup and adjust the seasoning with additional salt and pepper if needed.
- **Serve:**
  - Remove the bay leaf before serving. Ladle the hearty lentil soup into bowls, garnish with fresh parsley, and serve with lemon wedges on the side.
- **Enjoy:**
  - Squeeze a bit of fresh lemon juice into the soup before eating for a burst of citrusy flavor.

CREAMY BUTTERNUT SQUASH AND SAGE SOUP

Ingredients:
- 1 medium butternut squash, peeled, seeded, and diced
- 1 onion, chopped
- 2 carrots, peeled and chopped
- 2 celery stalks, chopped
- 2 cloves garlic, minced
- 4 cups vegetable broth
- 1/2 cup heavy cream
- 2 tablespoons olive oil
- 1 tablespoon fresh sage leaves, chopped
- Salt and pepper to taste
- Pumpkin seeds for garnish

Instructions:
1. **Sauté Vegetables:**
   - In a large pot, heat olive oil over medium heat. Add chopped onion, carrots, celery, and garlic. Sauté until the vegetables are softened.
2. **Add Butternut Squash:**
   - Add diced butternut squash to the pot. Stir and cook for an additional 5 minutes.
3. **Simmer Soup:**
   - Pour in vegetable broth and bring the mixture to a simmer. Cook until the butternut squash is tender.
4. **Blend:**
   - Using an immersion blender or transferring to a blender in batches, blend the soup until smooth.
5. **Add Cream and Sage:**
   - Return the soup to the pot. Stir in heavy cream and chopped fresh sage. Season with salt and pepper to taste.
6. **Serve and Garnish:**
   - Ladle the creamy butternut squash and sage soup into bowls. Garnish with pumpkin seeds before serving.

MAPLE BALSAMIC GLAZED BRUSSELS SPROUTS

Ingredients:
- 1 pound Brussels sprouts, trimmed and halved
- 3 tablespoons olive oil
- 2 tablespoons balsamic vinegar
- 2 tablespoons maple syrup
- 1/4 cup pecans, chopped
- Salt and black pepper to taste
- Grated Parmesan cheese for garnish

Instructions:

1. **Roast Brussels Sprouts:**
   - Preheat your oven to 400°F (200°C). Toss halved Brussels sprouts with olive oil, salt, and pepper. Roast in the oven for 20-25 minutes or until they are golden brown and crispy.
2. **Prepare Glaze:**
   - In a small saucepan, heat balsamic vinegar and maple syrup over medium heat. Simmer for a few minutes until it thickens slightly.
3. **Glaze Brussels Sprouts:**
   - Drizzle the balsamic maple glaze over the roasted Brussels sprouts. Toss to coat evenly.
4. **Add Pecans and Serve:**
   - Sprinkle chopped pecans over the Brussels sprouts. Transfer to a serving dish and garnish with grated Parmesan cheese. Serve warm.

HERB-INFUSED PUMPKIN SOUP

Ingredients:
- 1 medium pumpkin, peeled, seeded, and diced
- 1 onion, chopped
- 2 carrots, peeled and chopped
- 3 cloves garlic, minced
- 4 cups vegetable broth
- 1 cup coconut milk
- 2 tablespoons olive oil
- 1 teaspoon fresh thyme leaves
- 1 teaspoon fresh sage leaves, chopped
- Salt and pepper to taste
- Pumpkin seeds for garnish

Instructions:

1. **Sauté Vegetables:**
   - In a large pot, heat olive oil over medium heat. Add chopped onion, carrots, and garlic. Sauté until the vegetables are softened.

2. **Add Pumpkin:**
   - Add diced pumpkin to the pot. Stir and cook for an additional 5 minutes.

3. **Simmer Soup:**
   - Pour in vegetable broth and bring the mixture to a simmer. Cook until the pumpkin is tender.

4. **Blend:**
   - Using an immersion blender or transferring to a blender in batches, blend the soup until smooth.

5. **Add Coconut Milk and Herbs:**
   - Return the soup to the pot. Stir in coconut milk, fresh thyme, and chopped sage. Season with salt and pepper to taste.

6. **Serve and Garnish:**
   - Ladle the herb-infused pumpkin soup into bowls. Garnish with pumpkin seeds before serving.

HONEY LAVENDER ROASTED CHICKEN

Ingredients:
- 1 whole chicken (about 4-5 pounds)
- 1/4 cup honey
- 2 tablespoons dried culinary lavender
- 2 tablespoons olive oil
- 2 tablespoons balsamic vinegar
- Salt and black pepper to taste
- Fresh lavender sprigs for garnish (optional)

Instructions:
1. **Preheat Oven:**
   - Preheat your oven to 375°F (190°C).
2. **Prepare Chicken:**
   - Rinse the whole chicken and pat it dry with paper towels. Season the chicken inside and out with salt and black pepper.
3. **Make Honey Lavender Glaze:**
   - In a small bowl, mix honey, dried lavender, olive oil, and balsamic vinegar to create the glaze.
4. **Brush and Roast:**
   - Place the seasoned chicken in a roasting pan. Brush the chicken with the honey lavender glaze, ensuring it's evenly coated.
5. **Roast Until Golden:**
   - Roast the chicken in the preheated oven for about 1 hour and 30 minutes or until the internal temperature reaches 165°F (74°C). Baste the chicken with the glaze every 30 minutes.
6. **Rest and Garnish:**
   - Let the roasted chicken rest for 10-15 minutes before carving. Optionally, garnish with fresh lavender sprigs for a charming presentation.

SAGE AND CRANBERRY STUFFED PORK CHOPS

Ingredients:
- 4 thick-cut pork chops
- 1 cup breadcrumbs
- 1/2 cup dried cranberries, chopped
- 1/4 cup fresh sage leaves, chopped
- 1/4 cup pecans, chopped
- Salt and pepper to taste
- 2 tablespoons olive oil
- 1 cup chicken broth
- 2 tablespoons butter

Instructions:
1. **Preheat Oven:**
   - Preheat your oven to 375°F (190°C).
2. **Prepare Stuffing:**
   - In a bowl, mix breadcrumbs, dried cranberries, fresh sage, chopped pecans, salt, and pepper.
3. **Create Pocket:**
   - Cut a slit in each pork chop to create a pocket. Stuff each pocket with the breadcrumb mixture.
4. **Season and Sear:**
   - Season the stuffed pork chops with salt and pepper. In an oven-safe skillet, heat olive oil over medium-high heat. Sear the pork chops until browned on both sides.
5. **Add Broth and Roast:**
   - Pour chicken broth into the skillet. Transfer the skillet to the preheated oven and roast for about 20-25 minutes or until the internal temperature reaches 145°F (63°C).
6. **Finish with Butter:**
   - During the last few minutes of roasting, add butter to the skillet, allowing it to melt and baste the pork chops.
7. **Rest and Serve:**
   - Let the stuffed pork chops rest for a few minutes before serving.

ROSEMARY GARLIC ROAST CHICKEN

Ingredients:
- 1 whole chicken (about 4-5 pounds)
- 4 cloves garlic, minced
- 2 tablespoons fresh rosemary, chopped
- 2 tablespoons olive oil
- Salt and black pepper to taste
- 1 lemon, halved
- 1 onion, quartered
- 4 carrots, peeled and halved
- 4 potatoes, scrubbed and quartered

Instructions:
1. **Preheat Oven:**
   - Preheat your oven to 425°F (220°C).
2. **Prepare Chicken:**
   - Pat the chicken dry with paper towels. Mix minced garlic, chopped rosemary, olive oil, salt, and pepper to create a paste. Rub the paste all over the chicken.
3. **Stuff and Arrange:**
   - Place the lemon halves inside the chicken cavity. Arrange the chicken in a roasting pan surrounded by onion, carrots, and potatoes.
4. **Roast:**
   - Roast in the preheated oven for about 1 hour or until the chicken reaches an internal temperature of 165°F (74°C).
5. **Rest and Carve:**
   - Allow the chicken to rest for 10 minutes before carving. Serve with roasted vegetables.

CRANBERRY PECAN STUFFED ACORN SQUASH

Ingredients:
- 2 acorn squash, halved and seeds removed
- 1 cup quinoa, cooked
- 1/2 cup dried cranberries
- 1/2 cup pecans, chopped
- 1/4 cup fresh parsley, chopped
- 2 tablespoons maple syrup
- 2 tablespoons olive oil
- Salt and pepper to taste

Instructions:
1. **Preheat Oven:**
   - Preheat your oven to 375°F (190°C).
2. **Roast Acorn Squash:**
   - Place acorn squash halves on a baking sheet, cut side up. Drizzle with olive oil and season with salt and pepper. Roast for 30-35 minutes or until tender.
3. **Prepare Quinoa Filling:**
   - In a bowl, combine cooked quinoa, dried cranberries, chopped pecans, fresh parsley, maple syrup, olive oil, salt, and pepper.
4. **Stuff Squash:**
   - Fill each roasted acorn squash half with the quinoa mixture.
5. **Bake Again:**
   - Return the stuffed squash to the oven and bake for an additional 10-15 minutes.
6. **Serve Warm:**
   - Once heated through, serve the cranberry pecan stuffed acorn squash warm.

HOMESTEAD CHICKEN SOUP

Ingredients:

- 1 whole chicken (about 4-5 pounds), giblets removed
- 8 cups chicken broth
- 2 carrots, peeled and sliced
- 2 celery stalks, sliced
- 1 onion, diced
- 3 cloves garlic, minced
- 1 cup potatoes, diced
- 1 cup butternut squash, diced
- 1 cup green beans, chopped
- 1 cup corn kernels (fresh or frozen)
- 1 bay leaf
- 1 teaspoon dried thyme
- Salt and black pepper to taste
- Fresh parsley for garnish

Instructions:

- **Prepare the Chicken:**
  - Rinse the whole chicken under cold water and pat it dry with paper towels. Season the chicken with salt and pepper.
- **Boil the Chicken:**
  - In a large pot, bring the chicken and chicken broth to a boil. Reduce the heat to simmer and cook for about 1 hour or until the chicken is cooked through.

- **Remove Chicken:**
  - Carefully remove the cooked chicken from the pot. Let it cool slightly, then shred the meat from the bones. Discard the bones and skin.
- **Add Vegetables:**
  - To the pot with the broth, add carrots, celery, onion, garlic, potatoes, butternut squash, green beans, corn, bay leaf, and dried thyme. Simmer until the vegetables are tender, about 20-25 minutes.
- **Add Shredded Chicken:**
  - Add the shredded chicken back to the pot. Simmer for an additional 10 minutes to allow the flavors to meld.
- **Season and Garnish:**
  - Season the soup with salt and black pepper to taste. Remove the bay leaf. Garnish with fresh parsley just before serving.
- **Serve Warm:**
  - Ladle the homestead chicken soup into bowls. Serve warm with crusty bread for a wholesome and satisfying meal.

BREADS & SPREADS

HOMESTEAD DINNER ROLLS

Ingredients:
- 1 cup warm milk (about 110°F/43°C)
- 2 tablespoons sugar
- 2 1/4 teaspoons (1 packet) active dry yeast
- 3 1/2 cups all-purpose flour
- 1/4 cup unsalted butter, softened
- 1 teaspoon salt
- 1 large egg, beaten (for egg wash)
- Sesame seeds or poppy seeds for topping (optional)

Instructions:

- Activate Yeast:
  - In a bowl, combine warm milk and sugar. Sprinkle the active dry yeast over the mixture. Let it sit for 5-10 minutes until it becomes frothy.
- Mix Dough:
  - In a large mixing bowl, combine the flour, softened butter, and salt. Pour in the activated yeast mixture. Mix until a dough forms.
- Knead Dough:
  - Turn the dough out onto a floured surface and knead for about 8-10 minutes or until it becomes smooth and elastic.

- First Rise:
  - Place the dough in a greased bowl, cover it with a clean kitchen towel, and let it rise in a warm place for 1-1.5 hours or until it has doubled in size.
- Shape Rolls:
  - Punch down the risen dough and divide it into 12 equal portions. Shape each portion into a ball and place them in a greased baking pan, leaving a small gap between each roll.
- Second Rise:
  - Cover the pan with a kitchen towel and let the rolls rise for an additional 30-45 minutes.
- Preheat Oven:
  - Preheat your oven to 375°F (190°C).
- Brush with Egg Wash:
  - Beat the egg and brush it over the tops of the risen rolls. This gives them a beautiful golden color when baked. Optionally, sprinkle sesame seeds or poppy seeds on top.
- Bake:
  - Bake the rolls in the preheated oven for 15-20 minutes or until they are golden brown on top.
- Serve Warm:
  - Allow the dinner rolls to cool for a few minutes before serving. Enjoy these soft and fluffy homestead dinner rolls with your favorite meals.

HONEY OAT BREAD

Ingredients:

- 1 cup warm milk (about 110°F/43°C)
- 2 tablespoons unsalted butter, melted
- 2 tablespoons honey
- 1 cup rolled oats
- 3 cups all-purpose flour
- 2 1/4 teaspoons (1 packet) active dry yeast
- 1 teaspoon salt
- Extra oats for sprinkling (optional)

Instructions:

- **Activate the Yeast:**
  - In a small bowl, combine the warm milk, honey, and yeast. Stir gently and let it sit for about 5-10 minutes until the mixture is frothy.
- **Prepare the Oats:**
  - In a separate bowl, pour the warm melted butter over the rolled oats. Mix well and let them sit for 5-10 minutes to absorb the butter.
- **Mix the Dough:**
  - In a large mixing bowl, combine the flour and salt. Add the activated yeast mixture and the oats mixture.
  - Stir everything together until a rough dough forms.
- **Knead the Dough:**
  - Turn the dough out onto a floured surface and knead for about 8-10 minutes until it becomes smooth and elastic. Add more flour if the dough is too sticky.

- **First Rise:**
  - Place the dough in a greased bowl, cover it with a kitchen towel, and let it rise in a warm place for 1-1.5 hours, or until it has doubled in size.
- **Shape the Loaf:**
  - Punch down the risen dough and turn it out onto a floured surface.
  - Shape the dough into a rectangle and then roll it into a log, tucking the ends underneath.
- **Second Rise:**
  - Place the shaped dough in a greased loaf pan. Cover it with a kitchen towel and let it rise for an additional 30-45 minutes.
- **Preheat the Oven:**
  - Preheat your oven to 350°F (175°C).
- **Bake:**
  - Optionally, brush the top of the loaf with water and sprinkle extra oats for a rustic appearance.
  - Bake in the preheated oven for 30-35 minutes or until the bread has a golden-brown crust and sounds hollow when tapped.
- **Cool:**
  - Allow the bread to cool in the pan for 10 minutes, then transfer it to a wire rack to cool completely before slicing.

Enjoy your homemade Honey Oat Bread! It's perfect for toasting, making sandwiches, or simply spreading with butter for a delicious treat.

SOURDOUGH BREAD

Ingredients

For the Sourdough Starter:
- 1/2 cup all-purpose flour
- 1/4 cup whole wheat flour
- 1/2 cup lukewarm water

For the Bread Dough:
- 1 cup active sourdough starter
- 3 cups all-purpose flour
- 1 1/2 teaspoons salt
- 1 cup lukewarm water

Instructions:

Day 1: Create the Sourdough Starter

- **Mixing the Starter:**
  - In a glass or plastic container, mix 1/2 cup all-purpose flour, 1/4 cup whole wheat flour, and 1/2 cup lukewarm water. Stir until well combined.

- **Feeding the Starter:**
  - Cover the container loosely and let it sit at room temperature (around 70°F/21°C) for 24 hours.

Day 2: Continue Feeding the Starter

- **Feed the Starter:**
  - Add another 1/2 cup all-purpose flour and 1/4 cup lukewarm water to the starter. Stir well and let it sit for another 24 hours.

Day 3: Starter Should Be Bubbly

- **Check for Bubbles:**
  - By now, your starter should be bubbly and have a pleasant, slightly tangy smell. If it's not quite there, continue the feeding process for another day or two.

Day 4: Final Starter Feeding

- **Feed the Starter One Last Time:**
  - Add 1/2 cup all-purpose flour and 1/4 cup lukewarm water to the starter. Stir well and let it sit for 4-6 hours.

Day 5: Making the Bread

- **Preparing the Dough:**
  - In a large mixing bowl, combine 1 cup of the active sourdough starter, 3 cups all-purpose flour, salt, and 1 cup lukewarm water. Mix until a shaggy dough forms.
- **Kneading the Dough:**
  - Turn the dough onto a floured surface and knead for about 10-15 minutes until it becomes smooth and elastic.
- **First Rise:**
  - Place the dough in a greased bowl, cover with a damp cloth, and let it rise at room temperature for 4-8 hours, or until it has doubled in size.

- Shaping the Loaf:
  - Turn the dough onto a floured surface, shape it into a round loaf, and place it in a well-floured proofing basket or bowl, seam side down.
- Second Rise:
  - Cover the shaped loaf and let it rise for another 4-8 hours or until it has doubled in size.
- Preheat the Oven:
  - Preheat your oven to 450°F (232°C). Place a Dutch oven with a lid inside the oven while it preheats.
- Bake:
  - Carefully transfer the risen dough into the preheated Dutch oven. Score the top with a sharp knife. Cover with the lid and bake for 30 minutes. Remove the lid and bake for an additional 15-20 minutes or until the bread has a golden-brown crust.
- Cool:
  - Allow the sourdough bread to cool on a wire rack before slicing.

Enjoy the process of creating your sourdough bread from scratch, and savor the wonderful flavors of this homemade, naturally leavened loaf!

H O M E M A D E
B U T T E R

Ingredients:

- Heavy cream (preferably at room temperature)

Instructions:

- **Pour the Cream:**
  - Pour the heavy cream into the bowl of a stand mixer fitted with the whisk attachment.

- **Whip the Cream:**
  - Whip the cream on medium-high speed. Initially, it will form whipped cream with soft peaks.

- **Continue Whipping:**
  - Keep whipping the cream. It will go through several stages, starting with soft peaks, progressing to stiff peaks, and then separating into butterfat and buttermilk.

- **Separate Buttermilk:**
  - Once you notice a clear separation between the butterfat and buttermilk, stop the mixer.

- **Strain the Mixture:**
  - Strain the mixture to separate the butter and buttermilk. Save the buttermilk for other recipes.

- Rinse the Butter:

  - Rinse the butter under cold water while gently kneading it. This helps remove any remaining buttermilk, preventing the butter from turning rancid too quickly.

- Salt (Optional):
  - If you desire salted butter, knead in a pinch of salt to taste.

- Shape and Refrigerate:

  - Shape the butter into a log, ball, or use butter molds if you have them.
  - Wrap the butter in parchment paper or plastic wrap and refrigerate.

- Enjoy:
  - Your homemade butter is ready to spread on warm bread or use in your favorite recipes.

Feel free to experiment with this basic recipe by adding herbs, honey, or other flavorings to create unique variations of homemade butter. Enjoy the satisfaction of creating your own creamy butter from scratch!

DANDELION HONEY WALNUT BREAD

Ingredients:

- 2 cups dandelion petals (washed and separated from green parts)
- 2 cups all-purpose flour
- 1 teaspoon baking powder
- 1/2 teaspoon baking soda
- 1/2 teaspoon salt
- 1 teaspoon ground cinnamon
- 1/2 cup unsalted butter, softened
- 1/2 cup honey
- 2 large eggs
- 1 teaspoon vanilla extract
- 1/2 cup plain Greek yogurt
- 1 cup chopped walnuts

Instructions:

- **Prepare Dandelion Petals:**
  - Wash the dandelion petals thoroughly, ensuring they are free from green parts. Pat them dry.
- **Preheat Oven:**
  - Preheat your oven to 350°F (175°C). Grease and flour a loaf pan.
- **Mix Dry Ingredients:**
  - In a bowl, whisk together the flour, baking powder, baking soda, salt, and ground cinnamon.

- **Cream Butter and Honey:**
  - In a separate large bowl, cream together the softened butter and honey until smooth.
- **Add Eggs and Vanilla:**
  - Beat in the eggs one at a time, then stir in the vanilla extract.
- **Alternate Wet and Dry Ingredients:**
  - Gradually add the dry ingredients to the wet ingredients, alternating with the Greek yogurt. Begin and end with the dry ingredients. Mix until just combined.
- **Fold in Dandelion Petals and Walnuts:**
  - Gently fold in the dandelion petals and chopped walnuts into the batter.
- **Bake:**
  - Pour the batter into the prepared loaf pan.
  - Bake in the preheated oven for 55-65 minutes or until a toothpick inserted into the center comes out clean.
- **Cool:**
  - Allow the dandelion bread to cool in the pan for 10 minutes before transferring it to a wire rack to cool completely.
- **Slice and Enjoy:**

Once cooled, slice the Dandelion Honey Walnut Bread and relish the harmonious blend of flavors.

MAPLE WALNUT BUTTER

- 1 cup unsalted butter, softened
- 1/4 cup pure maple syrup
- 1/2 cup chopped walnuts
- Pinch of salt

Instructions:
- Beat butter until creamy. Add maple syrup, chopped walnuts, and salt.
- Mix until well combined. Refrigerate until firm.
- Spread on warm bread or muffins.

BERRY JAM DELIGHT

Ingredients:

- 3 cups mixed berries (strawberries, blueberries, raspberries)
- 1 cup granulated sugar (adjust based on your sweetness preference)
- 1 tablespoon lemon juice
- 1 teaspoon vanilla extract
- Pinch of salt

Instructions:

1. **Prepare the Berries:**
   - Wash and hull the strawberries. If using larger berries, chop them into smaller pieces.
   - In a medium-sized saucepan, combine the mixed berries.
2. **Cook the Berries:**
   - Over medium heat, cook the berries until they start to release their juices, stirring occasionally.
3. **Add Sugar and Lemon Juice:**
   - Stir in the granulated sugar and lemon juice.
   - Continue cooking over medium heat, allowing the mixture to simmer and thicken. This may take about 15-20 minutes.
4. **Test for Doneness:**
   - To check if the jam is done, place a small amount on a cold plate. If it wrinkles when you push it with your finger, it's ready.
5. **Add Vanilla and Salt:**
   - Stir in the vanilla extract and a pinch of salt to enhance the flavors.
   - Taste and adjust the sweetness if needed.
6. **Cool and Store:**
   - Allow the jam to cool slightly before transferring it to sterilized jars.
   - Once cooled, seal the jars and refrigerate.

Usage:
- Spread on toast, English muffins, or pancakes for a delightful breakfast.
- Swirl into yogurt for a fruity and sweet treat.
- Use as a filling for cakes, cupcakes, or thumbprint cookies.
- Blend with cream cheese for a flavorful spread on bagels.

Enjoy the burst of berry goodness in every spoonful of this homemade Berry Jam Delight. Feel free to customize the blend of berries and adjust the sugar to suit your taste preferences. It's a wonderful way to capture the essence of cottagecore living in your kitchen!

SWEET
MOMENTS

ROSE PETAL AND RASPBERRY JAM THUMBPRINT COOKIES

- 1 cup unsalted butter, softened
- 1/2 cup granulated sugar
- 2 cups all-purpose flour
- 1/2 cup raspberry jam
- Dried rose petals for decoration

Instructions:

1. Preheat the oven to 350°F (175°C).
2. In a bowl, cream together butter and sugar until light and fluffy.
3. Add the flour and mix until just combined.
4. Roll the dough into small balls and place them on a baking sheet.
5. Use your thumb to make an indentation in each cookie.
6. Fill each indentation with a small spoonful of raspberry jam.
7. Bake for 12-15 minutes or until the edges are lightly golden.
8. Decorate with dried rose petals while the cookies are still warm.

RUSTIC BERRY GALETTE

Ingredients:

For the Crust:
- 1 1/4 cups all-purpose flour
- 1/2 cup unsalted butter, cold and cubed
- 1 tablespoon granulated sugar
- 1/4 teaspoon salt
- 3-4 tablespoons ice water

For the Filling:
- 2 cups mixed berries (strawberries, blueberries, raspberries)
- 1/4 cup granulated sugar
- 1 tablespoon cornstarch
- Zest of 1 lemon
- 1 tablespoon lemon juice

Instructions:
- **Prepare the Crust:**
  - In a food processor, pulse together flour, sugar, and salt.
  - Add cold, cubed butter and pulse until the mixture resembles coarse crumbs.
  - Slowly add ice water until the dough comes together.
  - Shape the dough into a disk, wrap in plastic, and chill for at least 30 minutes.

- **Prepare the Filling:**
  - In a bowl, toss together berries, sugar, cornstarch, lemon zest, and lemon juice.
- **Assemble the Galette:**
  - Preheat the oven to 375°F (190°C).
  - Roll out the chilled dough on a floured surface.
  - Transfer the dough to a baking sheet.
  - Pile the berry mixture in the center, leaving a border around the edges.
  - Fold the edges of the dough over the berries.
- **Bake:**
  - Bake for 35-40 minutes or until the crust is golden and the berries are bubbly.
  - Allow to cool before slicing.

WHOLESOME MAPLE WALNUT OAT BARS

Ingredients:

- 1 1/2 cups old-fashioned oats
- 1 cup whole wheat flour
- 1/2 cup chopped walnuts
- 1/2 cup melted coconut oil
- 1/3 cup pure maple syrup
- 1/4 cup honey
- 1 teaspoon vanilla extract
- 1/4 teaspoon salt

Instructions:

1. Preheat the oven to 350°F (175°C). Grease a baking pan.
2. In a bowl, combine oats, whole wheat flour, and chopped walnuts.
3. In a separate bowl, whisk together melted coconut oil, maple syrup, honey, vanilla extract, and salt.
4. Mix the wet ingredients into the dry ingredients until well combined.
5. Press the mixture into the prepared baking pan.
6. Bake for 20-25 minutes or until the edges are golden.
7. Allow to cool completely before cutting into bars.

This recipe captures the essence of rustic charm and wholesome ingredients. Enjoy creating these delightful treats!

HAZELNUT ESPRESSO TRUFFLES

Ingredients:

- 8 oz dark chocolate, finely chopped
- 1/2 cup heavy cream
- 2 tablespoons hazelnut spread
- 1 tablespoon instant espresso powder
- Finely chopped hazelnuts or cocoa powder for coating

Instructions:
1. Heat the heavy cream until almost boiling and pour it over the finely chopped dark chocolate.
2. Stir until the chocolate is melted and smooth.
3. Mix in the hazelnut spread and instant espresso powder until well combined.
4. Refrigerate the mixture until it's firm enough to handle.
5. Scoop out small portions and roll them into truffle-sized balls.
6. Roll each truffle in finely chopped hazelnuts or dust with cocoa powder.
7. Chill until ready to serve.

ROSEMARY-INFUSED HONEY ROASTED PEACHES

Ingredients:

- Fresh peaches, halved and pitted
- Honey
- Fresh rosemary sprigs
- Vanilla ice cream (optional)

Instructions:

1. Preheat the oven to 375°F (190°C).
2. Place the peach halves, cut side up, on a baking sheet.
3. Drizzle honey over each peach half.
4. Place a small sprig of fresh rosemary on top of each peach.
5. Roast in the oven for 20-25 minutes or until the peaches are tender.
6. Serve the honey-roasted peaches on their own or with a scoop of vanilla ice cream.

COZY
CONFFECTIONS

VANILLA LAVENDER CAKE

Ingredients:

For the Cake:
- 2 1/2 cups all-purpose flour
- 2 1/2 teaspoons baking powder
- 1/2 teaspoon salt
- 1 cup unsalted butter, softened
- 2 cups granulated sugar
- 4 large eggs
- 1 tablespoon vanilla extract
- 1 1/4 cups whole milk

For the Lavender Infusion:
- 1/4 cup dried culinary lavender
- 1/2 cup boiling water
-

For the Lavender Buttercream:
- 1 cup unsalted butter, softened
- 4 cups powdered sugar
- 1/4 cup whole milk
- 1 teaspoon vanilla extract
- 1 tablespoon lavender-infused water (strained from lavender infusion)

Instructions:
- **Preheat the Oven:** Preheat your oven to 350°F (175°C). Grease and flour three 8-inch round cake pans.
- **Make the Lavender Infusion:**
  - Steep the dried lavender in boiling water for about 15 minutes.
  - Strain the lavender, reserving the infused water.

- **Make the Cake:**
  - In a bowl, whisk together the flour, baking powder, and salt.
  - In a large mixing bowl, cream together the softened butter and sugar until light and fluffy.
  - Add the eggs one at a time, beating well after each addition. Stir in the vanilla extract.
  - Gradually add the dry ingredients to the wet ingredients, alternating with the milk. Begin and end with the dry ingredients.
  - Stir in 1 tablespoon of the lavender-infused water.
- **Bake the Cake:**
  - Divide the batter evenly among the prepared cake pans.
  - Bake in the preheated oven for 25-30 minutes or until a toothpick inserted into the center comes out clean.
  - Allow the cakes to cool in the pans for 10 minutes before transferring them to wire racks to cool completely.
- **Make the Lavender Buttercream:**
  - In a large mixing bowl, beat the softened butter until creamy.
  - Gradually add the powdered sugar, milk, vanilla extract, and the remaining lavender-infused water. Beat until smooth and fluffy.
- **Assemble the Cake:**
  - Once the cakes are completely cooled, spread a layer of lavender buttercream between each layer.
  - Frost the top and sides of the cake with the remaining buttercream.
- **Decorate (Optional):**
  - Garnish with dried lavender buds or edible flowers for a decorative touch.
- **Serve and Enjoy:**
  - Slice and serve the Vanilla Lavender Cake, savoring the delicate floral and sweet flavors.

CHOCOLATE-DIPPED ALMOND BISCOTTI

Ingredients:
- 2 cups all-purpose flour
- 1 cup granulated sugar
- 1 teaspoon baking powder
- 1/4 teaspoon salt
- 3 large eggs
- 1 teaspoon vanilla extract
- 1 cup whole almonds, toasted
- 4 ounces dark chocolate, melted

Instructions:
1. **Preheat Oven:**
   - Preheat your oven to 350°F (175°C). Line a baking sheet with parchment paper.
2. **Mix Dry Ingredients:**
   - In a bowl, whisk together flour, sugar, baking powder, and salt.
3. **Combine Wet Ingredients:**
   - In a separate bowl, beat the eggs and vanilla extract. Add to the dry ingredients, mixing until a dough forms.
4. **Add Almonds:**
   - Fold in the toasted almonds.
5. **Shape and Bake:**
   - Divide the dough in half and shape each portion into a log on the prepared baking sheet. Bake for 25-30 minutes.
6. **Slice and Toast:**
   - Allow the logs to cool slightly, then slice into biscotti. Place them back on the baking sheet and bake for an additional 15 minutes, flipping halfway through.
7. **Dip in Chocolate:**
   - Once cooled, dip one end of each biscotti into melted dark chocolate.

ROSEMARY LEMON OLIVE OIL CAKE

Ingredients:
- 2 cups all-purpose flour
- 1 1/2 teaspoons baking powder
- 1/2 teaspoon baking soda
- 1/2 teaspoon salt
- 1 cup granulated sugar
- 3 large eggs
- 1 cup extra virgin olive oil
- 1 cup buttermilk
- Zest of 2 lemons
- 1 tablespoon fresh rosemary, finely chopped

Instructions:
1. **Preheat Oven:**
   - Preheat your oven to 350°F (175°C). Grease and flour a bundt pan.
2. **Mix Dry Ingredients:**
   - In a bowl, whisk together flour, baking powder, baking soda, and salt.
3. **Combine Wet Ingredients:**
   - In a separate bowl, beat sugar, eggs, and olive oil until well combined. Add buttermilk, lemon zest, and chopped rosemary.
4. **Mix:**
   - Gradually add the dry ingredients to the wet ingredients, mixing until just combined.
5. **Bake:**
   - Pour the batter into the prepared bundt pan. Bake for 45-50 minutes or until a toothpick inserted comes out clean.
6. **Cool:**
   - Allow the cake to cool in the pan for 15 minutes before transferring it to a wire rack to cool completely.

PRESERVES AND SWEETS

HOMEMADE STRAWBERRY JAM

Ingredients:
- 4 cups fresh strawberries, hulled and halved
- 2 cups granulated sugar
- 2 tablespoons lemon juice
- 1 teaspoon vanilla extract (optional)

Instructions:

1. **Prepare Strawberries:**
   - Wash and hull the strawberries. Cut them into halves or quarters, depending on your preference.
2. **Combine Ingredients:**
   - In a large saucepan, combine the strawberries, sugar, and lemon juice. Stir well and let the mixture sit for 15-20 minutes to allow the sugar to dissolve and the berries to release their juices.
3. **Cook Jam:**
   - Place the saucepan over medium heat and bring the mixture to a boil. Reduce the heat to a simmer and cook for about 30-40 minutes, stirring occasionally, until the jam thickens.
4. **Test for Doneness:**
   - To check if the jam is done, place a small amount on a cold plate. If it wrinkles when touched, it's ready.
5. **Add Vanilla (Optional):**
   - Stir in vanilla extract if using, and remove the saucepan from the heat.
6. **Cool and Store:**
   - Allow the strawberry jam to cool slightly before transferring it to sterilized jars. Seal the jars and store them in the refrigerator.

APPLE BUTTER

Ingredients:
- 8 cups apples, peeled, cored, and chopped (a mix of sweet and tart varieties)
- 1 cup granulated sugar
- 1 cup brown sugar, packed
- 1 tablespoon ground cinnamon
- 1/2 teaspoon ground nutmeg
- 1/4 teaspoon ground cloves
- 1/4 teaspoon salt
- 1 tablespoon vanilla extract

Instructions:
1. **Prepare Apples:**
   - Peel, core, and chop the apples into small pieces.
2. **Cook Apples:**
   - In a large pot, combine the chopped apples, granulated sugar, brown sugar, cinnamon, nutmeg, cloves, and salt. Cook over medium heat until the apples are soft and the mixture thickens, stirring occasionally. This can take 1-2 hours.
3. **Blend:**
   - Use an immersion blender to blend the mixture until smooth. Alternatively, transfer the mixture to a blender, blend, and return it to the pot.
4. **Add Vanilla:**
   - Stir in the vanilla extract and continue cooking until the apple butter reaches your desired thickness.
5. **Cool and Store:**
   - Allow the apple butter to cool completely before transferring it to sterilized jars. Seal the jars and store them in the refrigerator.

ORANGE CARDAMOM MARMALADE

Ingredients:
- 4 large oranges
- 2 lemons
- 4 cups water
- 4 cups granulated sugar
- 1 tablespoon cardamom pods, crushed
- 1 teaspoon vanilla extract

Instructions:
1. **Prepare Citrus Fruits:**
   - Wash the oranges and lemons thoroughly. Cut them into thin slices, including the peels, and remove seeds as you go.
2. **Cook Citrus Slices:**
   - In a large pot, combine the citrus slices and water. Bring to a boil, then reduce heat and simmer for 40-50 minutes or until the peels are tender.
3. **Add Sugar and Cardamom:**
   - Stir in the granulated sugar and crushed cardamom pods. Continue to simmer, stirring occasionally, until the mixture thickens (about 30-40 minutes).
4. **Test for Doneness:**
   - To check if the marmalade is done, place a small amount on a cold plate. If it wrinkles when touched, it's ready.
5. **Add Vanilla:**
   - Stir in the vanilla extract and cook for an additional 5 minutes.
6. **Cool and Store:**
   - Allow the Orange Cardamom Marmalade to cool slightly before transferring it to sterilized jars. Seal the jars and store them in the refrigerator.

HOMEMADE APPLESAUCE

Ingredients:
- 6-8 apples (a mix of sweet and tart varieties)
- 1/2 cup water
- 1/4 cup granulated sugar (adjust according to taste)
- 1 teaspoon ground cinnamon
- 1 tablespoon lemon juice (optional, to prevent browning)

Instructions:

- **Prepare Apples:**
  - Wash, peel, core, and chop the apples into small chunks. If you prefer a chunkier applesauce, you can leave the peel on for added texture.
- **Cook Apples:**
  - In a large saucepan, combine the chopped apples, water, sugar, and ground cinnamon. If using, add lemon juice to help prevent browning.
- **Simmer:**
  - Bring the mixture to a boil over medium-high heat. Once boiling, reduce the heat to low, cover the saucepan, and simmer for 15-20 minutes or until the apples are tender and easily mashed with a fork.

- **Mash or Blend:**
  - Use a potato masher for a chunkier texture or a blender/immersion blender for a smoother consistency. Blend until you achieve your desired texture.
- **Adjust Sweetness:**
  - Taste the applesauce and adjust the sweetness by adding more sugar if needed. Keep in mind that the sweetness can vary based on the type of apples used.
- **Serve:**
  - Serve the applesauce warm or cold. You can enjoy it as a snack, a side dish, or use it as a topping for various desserts.
- **Store:**
  - Allow the applesauce to cool completely before transferring it to airtight containers. Store in the refrigerator for up to a week or freeze for longer storage.

SAVOUR THE SEASONS

APPLE CIDER DONUTS

Ingredients:

- 2 cups all-purpose flour
- 1/2 cup granulated sugar
- 1 teaspoon baking powder
- 1/2 teaspoon baking soda
- 1/2 teaspoon ground cinnamon
- 1/4 teaspoon ground nutmeg
- 1/2 teaspoon salt
- 2/3 cup apple cider
- 2 large eggs
- 1/4 cup unsalted butter, melted
- Vegetable oil for frying
- Cinnamon sugar for coating

Instructions:

1. In a bowl, whisk together flour, sugar, baking powder, baking soda, cinnamon, nutmeg, and salt.
2. In another bowl, whisk together apple cider, eggs, and melted butter.
3. Add the wet ingredients to the dry ingredients, mixing until just combined.
4. Heat vegetable oil in a deep fryer or heavy pot to 350°F (175°C).
5. Drop spoonfuls of batter into the hot oil and fry until golden brown.
6. Drain on paper towels and immediately coat in cinnamon sugar.

PEACH AND BERRY COBBLER

Ingredients:
- 4 cups fresh or frozen peaches, sliced
- 2 cups mixed berries (blueberries, raspberries, blackberries)
- 1 cup granulated sugar
- 1 tablespoon cornstarch
- 1 teaspoon vanilla extract
- 1 cup all-purpose flour
- 1 cup granulated sugar
- 1 teaspoon baking powder
- 1/2 teaspoon salt
- 1 cup milk
- 1/2 cup unsalted butter, melted

Instructions:
1. **Preheat Oven:**
   - Preheat your oven to 350°F (175°C).
2. **Fruit Filling:**
   - In a mixing bowl, combine peaches, mixed berries, sugar, cornstarch, and vanilla extract. Toss until the fruit is evenly coated. Transfer the fruit mixture to a baking dish.
3. **Cobbler Topping:**
   - In another bowl, whisk together flour, sugar, baking powder, salt, milk, and melted butter until smooth. Pour the batter evenly over the fruit.
4. **Bake:**
   - Bake in the preheated oven for 45-50 minutes or until the cobbler topping is golden brown and the fruit is bubbly.
5. **Serve:**
   - Allow the cobbler to cool slightly before serving. Serve with a scoop of vanilla ice cream if desired.

HARVEST PUMPKIN MUFFINS

Ingredients:

- 2 cups all-purpose flour
- 1 teaspoon baking powder
- 1/2 teaspoon baking soda
- 1/2 teaspoon salt
- 1 teaspoon ground cinnamon
- 1/2 teaspoon ground nutmeg
- 1/4 teaspoon ground cloves
- 1/2 cup unsalted butter, softened
- 1 cup granulated sugar
- 2 large eggs
- 1 cup canned pumpkin puree
- 1/2 cup buttermilk
- 1 teaspoon vanilla extract

Instructions:

- **Preheat Oven:**
  - Preheat your oven to 375°F (190°C). Line a muffin tin with paper liners.
- **Dry Ingredients:**
  - In a bowl, whisk together flour, baking powder, baking soda, salt, cinnamon, nutmeg, and cloves.
- **Cream Butter and Sugar:**
  - In a separate large bowl, cream together the softened butter and sugar until light and fluffy.

- **Add Wet Ingredients:**
  - Add the eggs one at a time, beating well after each addition. Stir in the pumpkin puree, buttermilk, and vanilla extract.
- **Combine and Fill Muffin Cups:**
  - Gradually add the dry ingredients to the wet ingredients, mixing until just combined. Spoon the batter into the muffin cups, filling each about 2/3 full.
- **Bake:**
  - Bake for 18-20 minutes or until a toothpick inserted into the center comes out clean. Allow the muffins to cool in the tin for a few minutes before transferring them to a wire rack to cool completely.

SPICED APPLE CRISP

Ingredients:
- 6 cups apples, peeled, cored, and sliced
- 1 tablespoon lemon juice
- 1/2 cup granulated sugar
- 1 teaspoon ground cinnamon
- 1/4 teaspoon ground nutmeg
- 1/4 teaspoon ground cloves
- 1/2 cup old-fashioned oats
- 1/3 cup all-purpose flour
- 1/3 cup brown sugar, packed
- 1/4 cup unsalted butter, chilled and cut into small pieces

Instructions:
1. **Preheat Oven:**
   - Preheat your oven to 350°F (175°C).
2. **Prepare Apples:**
   - In a large bowl, toss the sliced apples with lemon juice, granulated sugar, cinnamon, nutmeg, and cloves. Transfer the apple mixture to a baking dish.
3. **Topping:**
   - In a separate bowl, combine oats, flour, brown sugar, and chilled butter. Use your fingers or a pastry cutter to mix until the mixture resembles coarse crumbs.
4. **Assemble and Bake:**
   - Sprinkle the oat topping evenly over the apples in the baking dish. Bake for 40-45 minutes or until the topping is golden brown and the apples are tender.
5. **Serve:**
   - Allow the spiced apple crisp to cool slightly before serving. Serve warm with a scoop of vanilla ice cream if desired.

AUTUMN BUTTERNUT SQUASH AND SAGE PASTA

Ingredients:
- 1 butternut squash, peeled, seeded, and diced
- 2 tablespoons olive oil
- 1 onion, finely chopped
- 2 cloves garlic, minced
- Fresh sage leaves
- 1 pound pasta of your choice
- Salt and pepper to taste
- Grated Parmesan cheese for serving

Instructions:
1. **Roast Butternut Squash:**
   - Toss the diced butternut squash with olive oil, salt, and pepper. Roast in the oven until tender and slightly caramelized, about 25-30 minutes.
2. **Sauté Onion and Garlic:**
   - In a pan, sauté the chopped onion in olive oil until translucent. Add minced garlic and fresh sage leaves, cooking until fragrant.
3. **Cook Pasta:**
   - Cook the pasta according to package instructions. Reserve some pasta water.
4. **Combine and Serve:**
   - Toss the cooked pasta with the roasted butternut squash, sautéed onion, garlic, and sage. Add pasta water if needed for a creamy consistency.
5. **Season and Garnish:**
   - Season with salt and pepper. Serve with grated Parmesan cheese on top.

WINTER SPICED HOT CHOCOLATE

Ingredients:
- 4 cups whole milk
- 1/2 cup unsweetened cocoa powder
- 1/2 cup granulated sugar
- 1/4 cup brown sugar, packed
- 1/2 teaspoon ground cinnamon
- 1/4 teaspoon ground nutmeg
- 1/4 teaspoon ground cloves
- Pinch of salt
- 1 teaspoon vanilla extract
- Whipped cream and cinnamon sticks for garnish (optional)

Instructions:
1. **Heat Milk:**
   - In a saucepan, heat the milk over medium heat until it's warm but not boiling.
2. **Mix Cocoa and Sugars:**
   - In a bowl, whisk together cocoa powder, granulated sugar, brown sugar, cinnamon, nutmeg, cloves, and a pinch of salt.
3. **Combine and Whisk:**
   - Whisk the dry ingredients into the warm milk until well combined. Continue heating until the hot chocolate is steaming.
4. **Add Vanilla:**
   - Stir in vanilla extract.
5. **Serve:**
   - Pour into mugs and top with whipped cream. Garnish with a cinnamon stick if desired.

Made in United States
Troutdale, OR
09/23/2024

23079156R00058